Infamous Trials

CRIME, JUSTICE, AND PUNISHMENT

Infamous Trials

Bruce Chadwick

Austin Sarat, GENERAL EDITOR

CHELSEA HOUSE PUBLISHERS
Philadelphia

Frontispiece: *Lawyer Clarence Darrow makes a point during the Scopes trial, 1925.*

CHELSEA HOUSE PUBLISHERS

Editorial Director Richard Rennert
Art Director Sara Davis
Picture Editor Judy Hasday
Production Manager Pamela Loos
Senior Production Editor Lisa Chippendale

Staff for INFAMOUS TRIALS

Senior Editor John Ziff
Editorial Assistant Kristine Brennan
Designer Takeshi Takahashi
Picture Researcher Alan Gottlieb
Cover illustration Takeshi Takahashi

First Printing

1 3 5 7 9 8 6 4 2

Library of Congress Cataloging-in-Publication Data

Chadwick, Bruce.
Infamous trials / Bruce Chadwick; Austin Sarat, general editor.

   p. cm. — (Crime, justice, and punishment)
Includes bibliographical references and index.

ISBN 0-7910-4293-6

1. Trials—United States—Juvenile literature. 2. Criminal justice, Administration of—United States—Juvenile literature.
I. Sarat, Austin. II. Title. III. Series.
KF220.C49 1997
345.73'02—dc21
96-40311
CIP
AC

Contents

CRIME, JUSTICE, AND PUNISHMENT

Fears and Fascinations:

An Introduction to
Crime, Justice, and Punishment

By Austin Sarat

We live with crime and images of crime all around us. Crime evokes in most of us a deep aversion, a feeling of profound vulnerability, but it also evokes an equally deep fascination. Today, in major American cities the fear of crime is a major fact of life, some would say a disproportionate response to the realities of crime. Yet the fear of crime is real, palpable in the quickened steps and furtive glances of people walking down darkened streets. At the same time, we eagerly follow crime stories on television and in movies. We watch with a "who done it" curiosity, eager to see the illicit deed done, the investigation undertaken, the miscreant brought to justice and given his just deserts. On the streets the presence of crime is a reminder of our own vulnerability and the precariousness of our taken-for-granted rights and freedoms. On television and in the movies the crime story gives us a chance to probe our own darker motives, to ask "Is there a criminal within?" as well as to feel the collective satisfaction of seeing justice done.

Fear and fascination, these two poles of our engagement with crime, are, of course, only part of the story. Crime is, after all, a major social and legal problem, not just an issue of our individual psychology. Politicians today use our fear of, and fascination with, crime for political advantage. How we respond to crime, as well as to the political uses of the crime issue, tells us a lot about who we are as a people as well as what we value and what we tolerate. Is our response compassionate or severe? Do we seek to understand or to punish, to enact an angry vengeance or to rehabilitate and welcome the criminal back into our midst? The CRIME, JUSTICE, AND PUNISHMENT series is designed to explore these themes, to ask why we are fearful and fascinated, to probe the meanings and motivations of crimes and criminals and of our responses to them, and, finally, to ask what we can learn about ourselves and the society in which we live by examining our responses to crime.

Crime is always a challenge to the prevailing normative order and a test of the values and commitments of law-abiding people. It is sometimes a Raskolnikov-like act of defiance, an assertion of the unwillingness of some to live according to the rules of conduct laid out by organized society. In this sense, crime marks the limits of the law and reminds us of law's all-too-regular failures. Yet sometimes there is more desperation than defiance in criminal acts; sometimes they signal a deep pathology or need in the criminal. To confront crime is thus also to come face-to-face with the reality of social difference, of class privilege and extreme deprivation, of race and racism, of children neglected, abandoned, or abused whose response is to enact on others what they have experienced themselves. And occasionally crime, or what is labeled a criminal act, represents a call for justice, an appeal to a higher moral order against the inadequacies of existing law.

Figuring out the meaning of crime and the motivations of criminals and whether crime arises from defiance, desperation, or the appeal for justice is never an easy task. The motivations and meanings of crime are as varied as are the persons who engage in criminal conduct. They are as mysterious as any of the mysteries of the human soul. Yet the desire to know the secrets of crime and the criminal is a strong one, for in that knowledge may lie one step on the road to protection, if not an assurance of one's own personal safety. Nonetheless, as strong as that desire may be, there is no available technology that can allow us to know the whys of crime with much confidence, let alone a scientific certainty. We can, however, capture something about crime by studying the defiance, desperation, and quest for justice that may be associated with it. Books in the CRIME, JUSTICE, AND PUNISHMENT series will take up that challenge. They tell stories of crime and criminals, some famous, most not, some glamorous and exciting, most mundane and commonplace.

This series will, in addition, take a sober look at American criminal justice, at the procedures through which we investigate crimes and identify criminals, at the institutions in which innocence or guilt is determined. In these procedures and institutions we confront the thrill of the chase as well as the challenge of protecting the rights of those who defy our laws. It is through the efficiency and dedication of law enforcement that we might capture the criminal; it is in the rare instances of their corruption or brutality that we feel perhaps our deepest betrayal. Police, prosecutors, defense lawyers, judges, and jurors administer criminal justice and in their daily actions give substance to the guarantees of the Bill of Rights. What is an adversarial system of justice? How does it work? Why do we have it? Books in the CRIME, JUSTICE, AND PUNISHMENT series will examine the thrill of the chase as we seek to capture the criminal. They will also reveal the drama and majesty of the criminal trial as well as the day-to-day reality of a criminal justice system in which trials are the exception and negotiated pleas of guilty are the rule.

When the trial is over or the plea has been entered, when we have separated the innocent from the guilty, the moment of punishment has arrived. The injunction to punish the guilty, to respond to pain inflicted by inflicting pain, is as old as civilization itself. "An eye for an eye and a tooth for a tooth" is a biblical reminder that punishment must measure pain for pain. But our response to the criminal must be better than and different from the crime itself. The biblical admonition, along with the constitutional prohibition of "cruel and unusual punishment," signals that we seek to punish justly and to be just not only in the determination of who can and should be punished, but in how we punish as well. But neither reminder tells us what to do with the wrongdoer. Do we rape the rapist, or burn the home of the arsonist? Surely justice and decency say no. But, if not, then how can and should we punish? In a world in which punishment is neither identical to the crime nor an automatic response to it, choices must be made and we must make them. Books in the CRIME, JUSTICE, AND PUNISHMENT series will examine those choices and the practices, and politics, of punishment. How do we punish and why do we punish as we do? What can we learn about the rationality and appropriateness of today's responses to crime by examining our past and its responses? What works? Is there, and can there be, a just measure of pain?

CRIME, JUSTICE, AND PUNISHMENT brings together books on some of the great themes of human social life. The books in this series capture our fear and fascination with crime and examine our responses to it. They remind us of the deadly seriousness of these subjects. They bring together themes in law, literature, and popular culture to challenge us to think again, to think anew, about subjects that go to the heart of who we are and how we can and will live together.

*   *   *   *   *

Among the most dramatic moments in the story of crime, justice, and punishment is the criminal trial. Trials are structured around adversarial combat played out in front of a judge and jury. They resolve issues of fact within a framework of rules, presumptions, and burdens of proof that, for many people, are almost incomprehensible. Yet because someone's liberty, or even their life, may be at stake, they compel attention. As the recent criminal trial of O. J. Simpson showed, trials can become moments of fascination for the entire nation.

Infamous Trials provides a rich and well-documented story of trials, going back as far as the proceedings against the accused Salem witches, that have fascinated the American public and that have also left nagging doubts. This book explores the troubling gap between law and justice and notes cases in which errors were made and questions raised about the fairness of legal verdicts. *Infamous Trials* also shows the human dimensions of law played out on a grand stage, telling the stories of people whose lives were on the line and of the actors who decided their fates. And, in the end, it reminds us that the struggle for justice is ongoing and that in the struggle each of us has a role to play.

O. J. Simpson (right) looks on as three of his lawyers pore over a document during Simpson's controversial trial for the murders of Nicole Brown Simpson and Ronald Goldman. From left: Johnnie Cochran, Gerald Uelmen (standing), and Robert Shapiro.

Preface

I t was called "the trial of the century." O. J. Simpson, football great, actor, and TV personality, stood charged with the brutal 1994 murders of his ex-wife and her friend, and media scrutiny could hardly have been more intense. The trial, which was televised nearly every day, dominated news broadcasts, produced huge headlines in the mainstream and tabloid press, and was analyzed daily by lawyers and talk show hosts. Millions of ordinary Americans debated the case at home, at work, and in school.

In and out of the courtroom, controversy reigned. Simpson's lawyers, dubbed the "dream team" because they included some of the nation's most famous attorneys, accused police of incompetence, evidence tampering, and racism (Simpson is black; both victims were white). Prosecutors bitterly denounced the defense's tactics, claiming they merely distracted attention from the solid case against the defendant. More than once, the unblinking eye of the TV camera captured tempers boiling over.

Though they couldn't be shown on television, the jurors weren't immune from all the bitterness. Rumors swirled that the jury was deeply divided along racial lines, and, when the judge dismissed a succession of jurors for misconduct, some of them—like other figures involved in the case—sold their stories to the press.

After a year of controversy and spectacle, the prosecution and defense rested, and the case finally went to the jury. After only a few hours of deliberation, the jury reached a verdict. When, on the morning of October 3, 1995, the foreperson read that verdict—not guilty—to a hushed courtroom and a TV audience of millions, many Americans were stunned. Some believed that the jury hadn't taken enough time deliberating; others insisted that Simpson was acquitted because his team of high-priced lawyers had raised the prosecution's "burden of proof" to impossible levels. Still others said simply that race had been a factor in the verdict. Whatever the reality of Simpson's guilt or innocence, many observers believed that in the "trial of the century," justice had not been done.

The Simpson trial, though, was merely the latest "trial of the century." And, given the continuing controversy that surrounds the proceedings and the verdict, it seems destined to join the ranks of America's most infamous trials. From the 1690s to the present, America has periodically witnessed high-profile cases in which the ideal of justice has collided with the realities of an imperfect legal system. This book is about some of those cases. When they took place, the trials, spanning 300 years of American legal history, dominated the headlines, stirred up arguments, and often turned into public spectacles. They continue to be discussed today not only because they had profound effects on American society, but also because the issues they raised are still relevant and because in each case there is at least the suspicion that, in some way, justice was not completely served, often with tragic consequences.

In theory, only evidence presented in the courtroom during a trial may figure in the verdict. In practice, however, trials don't occur in vacuums, and sometimes outside influences do intrude. That is one of the common threads binding together the infamous trials in this book. For example, during the Salem witchcraft trials in 1692, hysteria over witches gripped the small Massachusetts town; during the Rosenberg atomic-espionage trial in 1951, hysteria over Communism gripped the entire nation. If race played a role in the O. J. Simpson case, it *was* the case against the Scottsboro Boys, nine black youths convicted by all-white juries of raping two white women in the Deep South. The Scopes "monkey trial," which centered on the legality of teaching a scientific theory that seemed to be at odds with the Bible, took place in a tiny, deeply Fundamentalist town in Tennessee. The trial of the Chicago Seven was held at the height of America's most divisive war ever and, in the eyes of government officials and defendants alike, presented an opportunity to publicize the case for or against U.S. involvement in Vietnam.

Media coverage also can affect judicial proceedings. Some observers believe that the presence of TV cameras at the Simpson trial affected the way witnesses acted. But any disruption in that courtroom pales by comparison to what took place during the trial of Bruno Richard Hauptmann, charged in the kidnapping and death of aviator Charles Lindbergh's son. Then, hundreds of photographers snapped pictures at will, spectators cheered Lindbergh's every appearance and departure, and the curious picnicked on courtroom benches during testimony.

The American trial is presided over by a judge, a person presumably of extensive legal training whose function is to ensure that the proper procedures are followed. Judges must make decisions regarding what evidence may be presented at trial, what lines of questioning lawyers may pursue, what instructions jurors are given. And they must determine what sentence a convicted defendant will receive. For a fair trial, the judge must be competent and impartial. But this isn't always the case. The conduct and competence of judges in several of the infamous trials discussed in this book have been called into question. The judges in the Salem witchcraft trials, for example, had no legal experience. The judge in the Rosenberg atomic-espionage trial—by some accounts ambitious for an appointment to the Supreme Court—improperly communicated with government agencies during the trial and meted out sentences that seemed overly harsh. George Washington, who presided over the court-martial of his friend Benedict Arnold, rejected the advice of his colleagues and showed imprudent leniency.

The American trial is an adversarial proceeding. Prosecutors argue the case that the defendant committed the crimes he or she is charged with. Defense lawyers probe for weaknesses in the prosecution's case. Both sides must present all of the evidence, and witnesses must swear on a Bible to tell the truth. As the witnesses are questioned and the evidence critically examined, the guilt of the defendant must be proved "beyond a reasonable doubt" or the defendant must be acquitted. This does not always ensure that the guilty are punished and the innocent set free. For one thing, the skill of the lawyers can be a more decisive factor than the quality of the evidence. Just as many observers feel that the prosecution bungled the O. J. Simpson case, the prosecution in another case discussed in this book, the trial of eight Chicago White Sox baseball players for throwing the 1919 World Series, was clumsy and amateurish. And when key confessions mysteriously disappeared, the players—some of whom had accepted money to lose the games—were acquitted. In addition, witnesses do not always tell the truth, as happened in several of the cases examined in this book, most notably the rape trials of the Scottsboro Boys.

The jury has always played a central role in American justice. Begun in England in the 13th century, jury trials were brought to the shores of America by the Pilgrims and became the backbone of the U.S. legal system. Everyone accused of a crime is entitled to a trial before a jury of his or her peers, or equals, who evaluate the evidence and ultimately decide whether the defendant's guilt has been proved beyond a reasonable doubt. Jurors, unlike judges and lawyers, are legal laypersons, and the fairness of their verdict hinges on their intelligence, common sense, and impartiality. Sometimes the shortcomings of a jury get in the way of the correct verdict. The Simpson jury, some observers argued, was confused by defense arguments about the potential unreliability of the DNA tests that, the prosecution claimed, identified the blood of the defendant mixed with the blood of the two victims at the crime scene, in Simpson's car, and at his house. During the Scottsboro Boys' initial trials, doctors who examined the "victims" soon after the gang rape was said to have occurred found no evidence of forced intercourse, yet the juries overlooked that fact. And at succeeding trials, juries voted to convict even though one of the two accusers admitted on the stand that the rapes had never occurred.

The O. J. Simpson case will not be America's last controversial trial. Every year, there are highly publicized murders, terrorist bombings, instances of government corruption, and other scandals. In some of those cases a judge may be incompetent, witnesses may lie, juries may be biased. Police may do shoddy work, and the press may distort and sensationalize. Politics may outweigh the search for truth. And Americans will once again wonder whether their legal system has provided a fair trial, cleared the innocent, and appropriately punished the guilty.

HYSTERIA: THE WITCHES OF SALEM

Eleven-year-old Abigail Williams, who lived with her uncle, a minister, in Salem, Massachusetts, began to act strangely during the cold winter of 1692. She started by running around her house flapping her arms like a bird and whispering, "Whish! Whish!" Then she got down on her knees, in front of her family, and went into convulsions. She grabbed her throat with one hand, pushing away some unseen demon with the other, and screeched that a witch was trying to strangle her. Next, she took the irons from the fireplace and threw them about the room. Then she ran into the fireplace and tried to fly up the chimney.

Her family and neighbors were startled. Soon other

Disorder in the court: In addition to being presided over by judges with no legal training, the Salem witchcraft trials were constantly disrupted by the outbursts and melodramatic displays of accusers—some of them acting possessed, as in this painting. Defendants never stood a chance.

Above: Puritan clergyman Cotton Mather, whose book about the reported possession of a New England family by witches inspired two young girls to concoct stories of witchcraft in Salem. Opposite page: The title page from Mather's The Wonders of the Invisible World, *an account of the Salem witch trials that includes suggestions for combating "the Terrible things lately done by the unusual and amazing Range of Evil-Spirits in New-England."*

children in town began following Abigail's example, wrestling with invisible forces, gasping for breath, staring for hours, jerking their heads. The children all told parents, civic leaders, and ministers the same thing: there were witches in Salem who were taking possession of them.

The reaction of the townspeople led to one of the most infamous chapters in the history of religion and law in America, ending with a series of witch trials that showed the horrors of mass hysteria and weak courts. When the Salem witch trials were finally ended by the angry governor of Massachusetts, 19 men and women and two dogs, all suspected of being witches—even the dogs—were executed, 55 people pled guilty to avoid execution, 100 more were put in prison, and an additional 150 were awaiting trial. All of them were brought to trial on wild charges made up by the town's children.

The Salem witch hunt started in the home where Abigail Williams lived with her cousin, nine-year-old Elisabeth, the Reverend Samuel Parris and his wife, and their slave Tituba, who was from Barbados and who talked about voodoo. There, sitting on a shelf, was a book by Cotton Mather, a well-known Boston minister, about the reported possession of the Goodwin family by witches in 1688. The two girls apparently read the book, because all of their initial symptoms were right out of it. They soon claimed that Tituba was the witch who was possessing them and that two elderly women in town whom they did not like, Sarah Good and Sarah Osborne, were also witches. All three were arrested and put in jail.

Tituba, believing a guilty plea would allow her to avoid hanging, said she was indeed a witch and that the two old women were too. She told a bizarre story about a tall, thin man with white hair in Boston who showed her a Devil's book with the names of nine Salem witches written down in it.

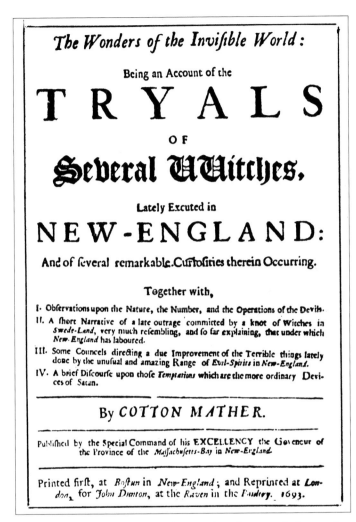

The Wonders of the Invisible World:

Being an Account of the

TRYALS

OF

Several Witches,

Lately Excuted in

NEW-ENGLAND:

And of several remarkable.Curtosities therein Occurring.

Together with,

I. Observations upon the Nature, the Number, and the Operations of the Devils.

II. A short Narrative of a late outrage committed by a knot of Witches in *Swede-Land*, very much resembling, and so far explaining, that under which *New-England* has laboured.

III. Some Councels directing a due Improvement of the Terrible things lately done by the unusual and amazing Range of *Evil-Spirits* in *New-England.*

IV. A brief Discourse upon those *Temptations* which are the more ordinary Devices of Satan.

By *COTTON MATHER.*

Published by the Special Command of his EXCELLENCY the Governcur of the Province of the *Massachusetts-Bay* in *New-England.*

Printed first, at *Boston* in *New-England* ; and Reprinted at *London,* for *John Dunton,* at the *Raven* in the *Pultry.* 1693.

That opened the floodgates for the witch hunt that followed. Dozens of teenage friends of Abigail and Elisabeth began to convulse and shout that witches were trying to bite them, twisted themselves into knots, and fell into trances. The children began to accuse dozens of people, including some of Salem's most-respected citizens, of witchcraft.

Witchcraft was not new. Several thousand people suspected of witchcraft in the 14th century were executed in different European countries. Witches played such a role in European culture that by the mid-1500s they appeared regularly in literature and plays, including William Shakespeare's *Macbeth*.

Trials for witches were not unusual either, particularly in England, the home of the settlers of Salem a generation before. As recently as 1600, 10 people suspected of witchcraft in Lancashire, England, had been hanged. People in Massachusetts frequently blamed sudden deaths or disasters on witches, so the idea of witches in Salem was not that strange in 1692.

The witch hunt picked up speed. The children were convinced they could have anybody jailed and began to target people. No one was safe. The next two arrested were Martha Corey and Rebecca Nurse, two highly respected elders of a local church, and five-year-old Dorcas Good, the daughter of jailed Sarah Good. Next was Mary English, the wife of a wealthy shipper. Then came George Burroughs, the town's former minister. Then it was John Alden, the son of one of the founders of the Massachusetts Bay Colony.

Critics complained that nearly all of the accused had at one time been involved in disputes with the children, their families, or others in Salem, and that the witchcraft arrests were retribution. No one listened.

The trials took on a life of their own. Seeing the hysteria that gripped Salem, many people began to confess to the crazy charges in order to avoid hanging, as Tituba did. One, Mrs. Deliverance Hobbs, confessed and then appeared in several trials as an acknowledged witch accusing many others of being witches.

The trials began on June 2, just after Massachusetts governor William Phips set out on a military campaign against Indians. He appointed a deputy governor, William Stoughton, and five other aides as judges for the witchcraft trials. None of them were lawyers, none had ever served as a judge, and none knew anything about the law. The judges soon became caught up in the hysteria. The defendants, many of whom were certain they would be acquitted, never had a chance.

The trial of Rebecca Nurse was typical of the way in which the proceedings were conducted. Eleven-year-old Abigail Williams, whose strange behavior continued throughout the spring and summer, was her chief accuser.

Judge: Have you seen this woman hurt you?

Abigail: Yes, she beat me this morning.

Just as Abigail finished, her friend, 12-year-old Ann Putnam, jumped up and yelled that Nurse had beaten her too.

Judge: Goody Nurse, here are two: Ann Putnam, the child, and Abigail Williams, complaining of your hurting them.

Nurse: I can say before my Eternal Father I am innocent, and God will clear my innocency.

A teenager, Henry Kenny, then jumped to his feet and said that he suffered two fits after Mrs. Nurse walked into his house. Ann Putnam's mother rose and backed up her daughter's story.

Judge: Here are not only these, but the wife of Thomas Putnam who also accuseth you.

Nurse: I am innocent and clear.

Ann Putnam's father then told the story of his daughter's convulsions, which he said were caused by the witch Goody Nurse. (*Goody* was the title for a married woman of lower rank.)

Judge: Is this true, Goody Nurse?

Nurse: I never afflicted no child, no never in my life.

Judge: Are you an innocent person relating to this witch-craft?

Before Rebecca Nurse could answer, Mrs. Putnam jumped up again and said that Nurse had brought a mysterious "black man" to her house and, pointing a finger at her, asked, "Did you not bid me tempt God and die?"

Massachusetts governor William Phips (pictured here) put an end to the Salem witch trials only after his own wife was accused of witchcraft.

Distraught, Nurse begged, "Oh Lord, help me . . ." As she spread out her hands before her, as if to plead for God's help, something strange happened that caused a gasp in the courtroom: all the children stretched their hands out the same way, and whatever Nurse did with her hands, they did with theirs.

Later, Nurse held her head to one side as another adult accused her of witchcraft. Everyone noticed that a maid who had also accused Nurse of witchcraft, Elizabeth Hubbard, kept her neck in the same position as Nurse's. Abigail Williams screamed to draw attention, pointed to Hubbard, and pleaded with the judge: "Set up Goody Nurse's head or the maid's neck will be broken!" Nurse was ordered to move her head up, and as she complied the maid also moved her head up. The townspeople were now convinced that Nurse was a witch.

Nurse's defense collapsed with the moving of the children's hands. Two stunned adults soon rose to accuse Nurse of bewitching them too, and other adults fell to the ground in seizures.

The judges and jury ignored any defense evidence in all the trials, no matter how strong it seemed. When a young girl claimed that Sarah Good broke a pair of scissors in half while stabbing her in the chest, a friend of hers stepped forward and told the court that they were his scissors and that he had broken them at her house doing repairs and had left them there. Sarah Good was found guilty. One woman's husband offered the court a testimonial signed by 39 of her neighbors that she was an admired woman and could not be a witch. It was ignored.

Even acquittals were reversed by the court. The jury found one woman not guilty, but the children began to scream and the judges ordered a new trial at which she was found guilty. Many pleaded guilty to escape death.

The first four "witches" were hanged on July 19 and the rest throughout the summer. Hundreds were incarcerated, and when the Salem jail was full, suspected witches were transported to jails in towns throughout the Boston area.

However, the trials outraged many people, including ministers and public officials, and the governor was pressured to end the witch hunt. The final straw came when the children of Salem accused the governor's own wife, Lady Phips, of witchcraft. The angry governor ruled that no one could be convicted of witchery based on testimony by self-confessed witches or invisible evidence. A special grand jury threw out charges against more than 100 of the accused in January 1693, and in February the governor reprieved those convicted and awaiting the gallows. He pardoned all the rest in May.

The pardons did not help Sarah Good, Rebecca Nurse, or the others hanged for witchcraft, but the public's disgust with what had taken place spurred change. The court system that permitted men with no legal training to sentence people to death was overhauled and dramatically improved, and a general reluctance to rely on the testimony of children grew.

American patriots prepare to burn a two-faced effigy of Benedict Arnold. Their belief that this will not be the traitor's last appointment with fire is underscored by the devil's pitchfork in Arnold's head.

THE COURT-
MARTIAL OF
BENEDICT ARNOLD

Every grade school student quickly learns that the greatest traitor in American history was Benedict Arnold, the American general who sold the secret plans to West Point—and plotted to turn over that strategic post—to the enemy during the American Revolution. The British officer he sold the plans to, Major John André, was caught and hanged, but Arnold escaped.

Though he never stood trial for treason, Arnold was earlier court-martialed for corruption. Those little-known proceedings, which took place in the middle of the war, showed his true character, and the verdict pushed him toward one of the greatest crimes in U.S. history.

Benedict Arnold was a genuine hero when he limped into Norris' Tavern in snow-covered Morristown, New Jersey, in

By 1779 Benedict Arnold had proven himself one of America's most capable and resourceful generals. Yet he never felt that his efforts were properly recognized, and his court-martial for corruption only deepened his bitterness.

December 1779 to face a court-martial board. His badly bruised leg was the result of but one of the injuries he had sustained in the fight for American independence.

Arnold was among the first soldiers to enlist in the Continental Army, organizing his own militia in Connecticut in 1775. He was an assistant commander to Ethan Allen, head of the Green Mountain Boys, during the stunning capture of Fort Ticonderoga, New York, that year. He led 1,100 men on a long march in brutal winter weather a few months later in an unsuccessful attempt to capture Quebec, where he was badly wounded.

Less than a year later, in 1776, Arnold showed his diverse talents when he supervised the construction of a small fleet of boats that attacked the much stronger British fleet on Lake Champlain and inflicted heavy damage. Then, risking his own life, he blocked British ships from chasing his fleet as it escaped.

In 1777 he led an army brigade that defeated the British near Danbury, Connecticut, and helped the Americans win the important battle of Saratoga. An impressed George Washington promptly made Arnold military commander of the city of Philadelphia.

However, throughout his entire career, Arnold, 38 at the time of his court-martial, felt that his efforts went unappreciated by his country and complained that he was never promoted quickly enough or given enough power. He called fellow generals bunglers.

Many in the army had no great admiration for him, especially since he lived lavishly while his men were quartered in huts. General Arnold was also disliked for marrying Peggy Shippen, a Loyalist (an American who supported the British in the war), and for being kind to her Loyalist friends.

He was accused of making illegal profits during the war by using his influence as a general; taking money for using his office to protect businessmen; improperly buying interests in cargo ships; giving legal protection to men who seized state-owned ships, and using army men and wagons to transport the ships' cargo; having the army shut down stores so he could secretly buy up their goods and then sell them at a profit; and general corruption and misconduct in office, including ordering his men to fetch barbers for his wife's servants.

Most of these charges were dismissed at a congressional hearing, but in December 1779, Pennsylvania leaders, led by John Reed, insisted that their charges of misconduct against Arnold be decided at a court-martial presided over by George Washington himself. Arnold, furious and hurt that his own country would put him on trial, rode to Morristown to face the court-martial board. His sense of being wronged comes through in a letter he wrote to the American people, which was published in dozens of newspapers:

> Conscious of having served my country faithfully for nearly four years, without once having my public conduct

impeached, I little expected . . . to be charged with crimes of which I believe few who know would have suspected me.

Arnold was court-martialed on only four charges: protecting men who had taken the cargo of government ships and profiting illegally from ships, misusing government wagons, selling goods he had bought from closed shops, and ordering soldiers to work for him.

General Arnold's defense showed clearly that he felt he was a patriot who had become a victim:

> When the present necessary war against Great Britain commenced, I was in easy circumstances and enjoyed a fair prospect of improving them. I was happy in domestic connections and blessed with arising family, who claimed my care and attention. The liberties of my country were in danger. The voice of my country called upon all her faithful sons to join in her defense. With cheerfulness, I obeyed the call. I sacrificed domestic ease and happiness to the service of my country and in her service have I sacrificed a great part of a handsome fortune. My time, my fortune, my person have been devoted to my country in this war. I was one of the first who appeared in the field and, from that time to the present hour, have not abandoned her service.

After the charges were read to him, Arnold stood bolt upright and, looking into the eyes of the 12 members of the court-martial board, said the accusations were "false, malicious and scandalous." Steadily and forcefully, he then explained away each charge in a comprehensive and impressive defense. His protection of the men who seized a ship, he said, was simply a mistake. He didn't know that they were making a profit from the war. He dismissed the charge of having a soldier (the son of one of Reed's friends) work for him by fetching a barber for his maid with a soaring speech about how thousands of soldiers throughout the army would do anything for a patriotic general, regardless of the task. He told the court he could not be tried on the charge of improperly profiting from the cargo of a ship because a civil court had found him not guilty. He said the wagons used for private gain were going to be paid for and, at the time, weren't needed for the protection of the public. He never bought goods from closed stores, he said, and demanded proof that he did (there was none because, it was charged, he had someone else actually buy the goods). He wound up his defense with an angry speech denouncing those from Pennsylvania who had brought the charges against him, particularly Reed, whom he accused of cowardice for resigning from the army when it appeared the Americans might lose the war in 1776.

Only a few witnesses testified, but what they said was damaging. John Mitchell was questioned about Arnold's role in making money by transporting a ship's cargo with army wagons. He said Arnold told him to

Arnold passes military secrets to John André, directing the British major to conceal the papers in his boots. Only André's chance capture prevented Arnold from surrendering the garrison at West Point to the English.

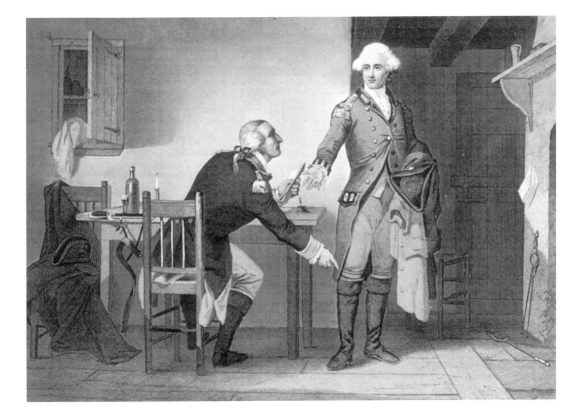

give him wagons owned by the state of Pennsylvania to remove goods from a ship. Colonel Charles Petit, a quartermaster in charge of wagons, said the same thing.

The army prosecutor questioned Petit and got him to admit that soldiers tended to do whatever generals requested. So did John Mitchell, another wagon officer.

> Prosecutor: Were the teams of wagons [drivers] employed by Arnold . . . as part of their detachment?
>
> Mitchell: As they were sent to General Arnold, I did not consider I had any charge of them, not confiding them to be in public service.
>
> Arnold (angry): Did you not tell me they were public wagons laying about town . . . they could be spared?
>
> Mitchell: I do not recall . . . .

Later, Major David Franks, one of Arnold's own aides, testified that he had orders signed by Arnold to shut down stores and buy up their contents for Arnold, but he had never acted on them.

Arnold thought his defense was good and that he had won. He had conducted himself so well, in fact, that he toyed with the idea of having the 179-page court-martial transcript published as a book and sold throughout the United States to show that he was a patriot, and he asked Washington to make him head of the navy.

Washington was extremely upset about the court-martial. The members of the board told him that not only should Arnold be found guilty of some of the charges, but he should be kicked out of the army. The charges, and even Arnold's defense, showed that the general was involved in criminal activities and that he didn't realize the importance of complete honesty for officers. There was much criticism of Arnold, from politicians as well as the public, and the criticism began to be leveled at the army itself, which weakened the war effort.

Following the board's recommendation, Washington found Arnold guilty of protecting the men who

seized the ship and of misconduct in the use of government wagons, but the sentence was nothing more than
a mild reprimand. He told Arnold:

> Even the shadow of fault tarnishes the lustre of our finest
> achievements. The least inadvertence may rob us of the
> public favor. You should have been guarded and temper-
> ate in your deportment towards your fellow citizens.

Washington did, however, very carefully word the
reprimand in the softest way, did not punish Arnold,
and even told him that he hoped Arnold's future
conduct in the army would redeem his image. George
Washington was convinced that Arnold would now
change his ways and become a better general. He was
wrong.

Benedict Arnold saw the reprimand as a betrayal by
his friend and commander and the final sign that no
matter how hard he fought for his country, his country
would never appreciate him. The court-martial pushed
him over the edge, into treason, and instead of being
remembered as one of the Revolutionary War's greatest
generals and a national hero, he wound up as perhaps
the most despised man in all American history.

JOHN COLLINS
Outfield

URBAN FABER
Pitcher

FRED McMULLIN
Infield

CLAUDE WILLIAMS
Pitcher

BYRD LYNN
Catcher

WHITE SOX
1919

EDDIE CICOTTE
Pitcher

RAY SCHALK
Catcher

"CHICK" GANDIL
First Base

WM. "KID" GLEASON
Manager

DICK KERR
Pitcher

"BUCK" WEAVER
Third Base

BILL JAMES
Pitcher

EDDIE COLLINS
Second Base

EDDIE MURPHY
Outfield

JOE JENKINS
Catcher

OSCAR FELSCH
Outfield

HARRY LIEBOLD
Outfield

"SWEDE" RISBERG
Shortstop

JOE JACKSON
Outfield

3.

Who "Fixed" the World Series?

Baseball has had many great teams, but few could compare with the 1919 Chicago White Sox. The White Sox won the World Series in 1917 and, after a disappointing season in 1918, were in the World Series again in 1919. They had baseball's two best pitchers in Eddie Cicotte, who won 29 games, and Lefty Williams, who won 23, and the game's best all-around player, Shoeless Joe Jackson. They were heavily favored to defeat the National League champs, the Cincinnati Reds, in the nine-game World Series and move into the 1920s as baseball's greatest dynasty.

To the utter astonishment of the sports world, however, the White Sox lost the series to the Reds, five games to three. One year later, as the White Sox were on their way to yet another World Series and Shoeless Joe Jackson was hitting .385, the nation was shocked when eight Sox players were charged with accepting bribes to "fix," or deliberately lose, the 1919 World

Baseball's "Black Sox." Eight of the men shown in this team portrait were accused of deliberately losing the 1919 World Series. Eddie Cicotte (second row, left) signaled gamblers that the fix was on by hitting Cincinnati's leadoff batter with his first pitch.

Series. Fans couldn't believe that baseball players could be bribed.

The players went on trial in Chicago, with thousands of fans jamming the courthouse each day. The verdict, and baseball's reaction to it, changed the face of baseball forever.

It was Jackson's teammate and friend, Chick Gandil, the Sox first baseman, who had approached two Boston gamblers, "Sport" Sullivan and "Sleepy" Burns, in September 1919 with the idea of fixing the World Series for $100,000. The players hated their owner, Charles Comiskey, who paid them salaries that were among the lowest in baseball and, they felt, treated them badly. Gandil was certain that he and others could pocket huge amounts of money by throwing games so that gamblers could make millions betting against the heavily favored team. He recruited Lefty Williams, Eddie Cicotte, Hap Felsch, Swede Risberg, Fred McMullin, and Buck Weaver.

Finally, there was Shoeless Joe Jackson (he had earned his nickname when he lost a shoe and kept playing). Jackson hit .351 in 1919 and was batting .356 lifetime, the third-highest average in the history of the game. Probably the best left fielder who ever lived (writers said his glove "was the place triples go to die"), he had such a strong arm that in the minor leagues he entertained crowds by standing at the base of the center field wall and throwing baseballs over the roof of the stadium behind home plate. He was also a clutch hitter and a good base runner.

But for all his remarkable gifts on the baseball diamond, off the field Jackson was an unusual and difficult man. Hot-tempered and impulsive, he constantly did things that annoyed people. He found it very hard to make and keep friends, had a short attention span, and had problems connecting actions with consequences (he would be surprised that someone he had just cursed out did not want to be his friend, for example). And

Jackson could barely read or write. At the time, he was considered just a poor illiterate. Today, he would be diagnosed as a learning-disabled person with social problems who would do anything to gain acceptance in a group. But as his teammates planned to throw the World Series, his strange personality made them wonder whether he would join them.

All the players except Jackson attended several meetings with the gamblers, who reportedly got their money from notorious New York gambler Arnold Rothstein. Six voted to go through with the deal, but Buck Weaver dropped out. According to grand jury testimony from Cicotte, Williams, and Jackson, all were paid at least $5,000 in stuffed envelopes before the first game and were promised more later. They told the gamblers that if Cicotte, the starting pitcher in the opening game at Cincinnati, hit the first batter, the fix was on.

Rumors about a World Series fix of some kind started just before the opening game. Enormous amounts of money were being bet on the underdog Reds by

Chick Gandil is thrown out trying to steal second base during the 1919 World Series. Rumors of a Series fix seemed to gain confirmation when the talented White Sox club made a host of errors and uncharacteristically inept plays.

unknown people. Players from teams not in the World Series told newspaper columnists that they'd heard the Series was fixed. Owner Charlie Comiskey heard that Joe Jackson had been at his office carrying a stuffed envelope and trying to see him but had been turned away. Then, on the day before the Series, Jackson found him in the ballpark and asked the owner to take him out of the lineup. Manager Kid Gleason kept seeing the same group of players, with strangers, having late-night meetings down the hotel hallway from his room.

The Series began on October 1, a clear, sunny day in Cincinnati. The stadium was packed. When the Reds' first batter, Harry Rath, stepped into the batter's box, he was hit in the back by Eddie Cicotte's first pitch. The fix was on, and the stage was set for the greatest scandal in the history of American sports.

The Reds won the first two games, 9-1 and 4-2, as the Sox made an incredible series of errors and batted poorly. The White Sox won the third game because Dickie Kerr, not part of the group throwing the games, pitched. Cincinnati won games four and five, and Chicago, again with Kerr on the mound, won game six. The White Sox won game seven, even though Cicotte was pitching, because Joe Jackson drove in the winning runs with a single in the late innings. The Reds won the eighth and final game, 10-5, with Lefty Williams pitching badly, even though Joe Jackson hit a titanic home run. Jackson had put on one of the greatest World Series performances in history, hitting a home run, batting .375, committing no errors, and making three sensational diving catches of line drives.

Rumors about a fix flew after the Series and during the 1920 season. The press demanded an investigation. Cicotte, Williams, and Jackson were called before a special grand jury in Chicago, hurried there with little notice in a move to pressure them into confessing. All three, Cicotte crying most of the time, admitted taking money to fix the Series and implicated all of the other players involved. Jackson, rambling in a two-hour interrogation, constantly changed his story and left attorneys puzzled about his involvement. At first he said he didn't participate.

> District Attorney: Didn't you think it was the right thing for you to go and tell Comiskey about it?
>
> Jackson: I did tell them once, I am not going to be in on it. I will just get out of that altogether.

Later, he seemed to say he was in on the fix.

> District Attorney: What did they say [about the fix]?
>
> Jackson: They said, "You might as well say yes or no and play ball or anything you want." I told them I would take their word.

The grand jury believed he was in on it. All eight players and some of the gamblers were indicted and ordered to stand trial, and Comiskey suspended the players. The news rocked the country.

Baseball's team owners were certain that the scandal would destroy the game. To clean their house and improve baseball's image, the owners took a bold step. They created the post of commissioner of baseball and hired a tough federal judge, Kenesaw Mountain Landis, to fill the position. His job was to make sure there was no more betting on games and to deal with the players, dubbed the "Black Sox" at the start of the trial, no matter what the verdict.

The trial began in June 1921 before a packed courtroom. It was front-page news all over the country, and sportswriters debated whether the game could survive the Black Sox scandal.

From the start, the trial was a legal mess. Buck Weaver, who never got any money and had nothing to do with the fix, had to stand trial anyway just because he went to the meetings. Although most of the gamblers involved were indicted, Arnold Rothstein was not, leading the press to speculate that he had bought his way out of jail. The prosecutors, so adept at getting

Notorious gambler Arnold Rothstein (pictured here) allegedly put up the money used to pay off the White Sox players. Yet he was never charged, leading to speculation that he had bribed authorities.

confessions out of the players in front of the grand jury, seemed amateurish in court and were often upstaged by the witnesses.

The courtroom was stunned during the first few hours when one of the gamblers, Sleepy Burns, pointed to Chick Gandil and, slowly and with great emphasis, said, "Gandil said, 'If I could get $100,000, I would throw the World Series!'"

The case soon became murkier. Cicotte, Williams, and Jackson took the stand for the defense and told surprised jurors that they were not represented by lawyers at the grand jury hearing, had no idea what documents prosecutors forced them to sign there, were never offered immunity, and now, looking back, thought what happened to them was illegal.

Jackson admitted that during his grand jury testimony he was drunk. He said he knew all about the fix, but never attended any meetings, tried to give back the money, and played his heart out during the Series. He said that if he hadn't played to lose and had tried to return the money, he couldn't have been part of the fix.

Then came the biggest bombshell of all. The grand jury confessions of Cicotte, Williams, and Jackson, which implicated everyone else, were mysteriously lost, sparking speculation that the gamblers paid off someone to steal them.

Without signed confessions and with testimony from notorious gamblers, the prosecution's case began to sag. Then, on the final day of the trial, it collapsed when the judge instructed the jury that it couldn't bring in a guilty verdict based merely on the fix:

> The State must prove that it was the intent of the ballplayers and gamblers charged with conspiracy through the throwing of the World Series, to defraud the public and others, and not merely to throw ballgames.

Veteran court workers were surprised that the jury returned with a verdict just a few hours later, at 10 P.M. All eight players were found not guilty. A roar went up

White Sox first baseman Chick Gandil had first approached two Boston gamblers in September 1919 with the proposition that his team throw the World Series in return for $100,000. At least part of his motivation was an intense hatred of team owner Charles Comiskey, a hatred shared by nearly all of Gandil's teammates.

from the crowd in the courthouse that was as loud as the cheers Shoeless Joe Jackson's home runs drew. The players hugged one another. They had been redeemed, and best of all, they could once again do what they loved most—play baseball.

Their joy proved short lived, however. Commissioner Landis, convinced that the men had fixed the Series and disgusted with the jury's decision, issued his own verdict as the players were celebrating in a Chicago restaurant. He said that in spite of the jury's not guilty verdict, he was banning the players from baseball for life.

Acquitted by a court of law, the White Sox players faced a harsh private punishment: they were banned from baseball for life. Perhaps saddest of all was the case of Shoeless Joe Jackson (shown here). The Sox outfielder hadn't attended any meetings with the gamblers, had attempted to return the money he was given, and had played spectacularly in the World Series.

Despite pleas, court challenges, and a personal appeal from Buck Weaver, Landis's decision stood. None of the eight ever played major league baseball again. Deprived of their reputations and their livelihoods, the men—including Weaver and Jackson, who no one felt fixed any games—were ruined. (Jackson was later immortalized in books, songs, poetry, and the popular movie *Field of Dreams*.)

Right or wrong, the baseball commissioner's tough stand had long-lasting effects on the game. Gamblers were barred from ballparks, and no more game-fixing scandals arose. The owners, impressed with Landis's take-charge attitude, gave him nearly unlimited power to run the game, and its newfound integrity, along with the emergence of Babe Ruth in 1920, not only permitted baseball to survive, but put it back on its feet and made it the national pastime.

The Great
Monkey Trial

Lawyer Clarence Darrow found what he saw on the morning of July 11, 1925, hard to believe. Along Main Street in tiny Dayton, Tennessee, banners urged people to read their Bible. Red, white, and blue bunting was draped from the rooftops of buildings. Large posters of monkeys were nailed to the sides of warehouses and taped to grocery store windows. People sold Bibles at intersections, and refreshment stands were set up every 50 yards. One man stood in a storefront window supervising a pair of dancing monkeys. Darrow, one of the country's most famous attorneys, smiled at the monkeys. That's why he too was in Dayton—for the "monkey trial."

The "monkey trial" was the trial of John Scopes, a substitute science teacher who was arrested for teaching evolution in a local school. Evolution, a theory developed by British scientist Charles Darwin, held that humans had evolved—over the course of millions of years—from lower animals, including monkeys.

45

Many Tennesseans were Fundamentalist Christians who believed in very strict interpretations of the Bible. The Bible said that God created man in a single day, so Darwin must be wrong. What's more, his theory went against religion. They favored the 1925 law their legislature had passed making the teaching of evolution in public schools illegal.

That law was challenged by the American Civil Liberties Union (ACLU), a national group. An ACLU lawyer convinced the 24-year-old Scopes to claim that he had taught evolution (actually, he had not) so the ACLU could make a national test case out of the clash between science and religion in public schools. So far, Tennessee was the only state with such a law (it failed to pass in four other states). The ACLU was fearful that Fundamentalists, and there were millions of them, would soon pass similar laws in many states and that the Christian religion would dominate public schools and curb the teaching of science and other subjects. Darrow was brought to Dayton because the prosecution had hired the noted leader of the American Fundamentalist movement and one of the most famous men in the world, three-time presidential nominee William Jennings Bryan. The promised battle between the two famous lawyers (neither charged a fee) turned the case into a media circus. More than 100 reporters jammed the courtroom, and WGN radio in Chicago carried the trial live on its nationwide radio hookup, a first.

At stake in the case was more than simply whether evolution could be taught in public schools. Among the important issues were: 1) Should the beliefs of any church dominate public education? 2) Freedom of speech: Wasn't Scopes protected by the First Amendment to the U.S. Constitution? 3) Could state laws override federal laws that protected individual rights? 4) Perhaps most important, what should happen when science and religion disagree? All the media attention (for its time, it resembled the O. J. Simpson trial) made

Charles Darwin's theory of evolution is parodied in this cartoon, as one of Homo sapiens' supposed ancestors comes calling in sartorial splendor.

the Scopes trial a huge national story that created front-page headlines every day.

The two famous lawyers, both in their late 60s, were imposing figures in the small courtroom in Dayton's old brick courthouse. Bryan was a large man with a thunderous voice who loved to talk and impressed everyone who listened. Darrow was a smaller, determined, well-dressed man who enjoyed sporting broad suspenders. He hammered away at witnesses with logical arguments. (Ironically, Darrow had worked for Bryan in two of his presidential campaigns.) Both men, and everyone in the courtroom, sweated in the hot summer of 1925.

The prosecution's case was simple: Since the legislature has the right both to make laws and to run the public schools, its antievolution law was constitutional. Bryan also argued that since religion could not be taught in public schools, evolution (or "evil-ution," as locals branded the theory on large signs they held up in the courtroom) should not be taught either.

The defense could have won the case in a single afternoon if it claimed that Scopes had never actually taught evolution, but it wanted victory on the larger national issue of religion and science in public education. So it argued that letting one religious group, Christians, decide what was taught in the state's schools was illegal; that the theory of evolution was scientifically valid; and, most important, that since there were many interpretations of the Bible, no single interpretation could be entirely truthful.

Darrow made a stirring speech to have the charges thrown out:

> Today it is the public school teachers, tomorrow the private. The next day the preachers and lecturers, the magazines, the books, the newspapers. After awhile . . . it will be creed against creed until, with flying banners and beating drums we are marching backward to the glorious ages of the sixteenth century when bigots . . . burned the men who dared to bring any intelligence and enlightenment and culture to the human mind.

The national press was very proevolution. The stories about the trial not only ridiculed Bryan, but also poked fun at the town, Judge John Raulston, and the people of Tennessee, whom reporters portrayed as simple bumpkins. Things were different inside the courtroom, however. Bryan and his assistants carefully carried on a campaign to paint Darrow and the ACLU as outsiders because they came from Chicago. The jury, all local residents of the small town, seemed very pro-Bryan. So did the judge, who paid no attention to the media and seemed to do everything he could to

The two principal adversaries in the Scopes trial, Clarence Darrow (left) and William Jennings Bryan, relax during a break in the proceedings. Within a week of Darrow's grueling cross-examination, Bryan was dead.

uphold the state law. A frustrated Darrow filed objection after objection, but the judge overruled most of them. Finally, the judge refused to let Darrow call any national experts on evolution, taking away his one chance to let the jury hear the other side of the evolution story. It appeared that the case was over.

Then Darrow had a brilliant idea. If he couldn't put anyone from his side on the stand, why not put someone from the other side on the stand and turn the tables? The next morning, he called William Jennings Bryan himself as a defense witness. A surprised Bryan gladly took the stand, waving to spectators and nodding knowingly to the jury, because he saw an opportunity to crush Darrow once and for all and to energize the entire nation with his religious zeal. (His friends, who knew Darrow and saw what was coming, begged Bryan not to testify.)

The trial was moved to the porch of the courthouse that morning because an engineer feared that the courthouse might collapse under the weight of the thousands of people who wanted to see the proceedings. Now, outside on a terribly hot day, Bryan, fanning himself furiously to beat the heat, had as his stage not only the courtroom, but the entire town, whose residents crowded around the porch on the courthouse lawn.

Darrow zeroed in on Bryan's deep religious beliefs right away, at first asking harmless questions about the Bible to lull the smiling Bryan into overconfidence. Next he got Bryan to say that the Bible was perfect and had to be interpreted exactly the way it was written. Then Darrow sprang his trap.

Did Bryan really believe that Joshua made the sun stand still, as the Bible said, and did he believe that nothing would happen to the earth if the sun stood still?

Bryan: I have never investigated the matter.

Darrow asked Bryan if he really believed that a whale, or "big fish," swallowed Jonah and that Jonah emerged, unhurt, after being inside the whale for a long time.

Bryan: Yes. God could make man and fish do what he wanted.

Darrow asked him if the brothers Cain and Abel were the only children of Adam and Eve. Bryan said they were. How, then, Darrow asked, did Cain, after he murdered Abel, find a wife and have children?

Bryan: I'll leave the agnostics [people who believe that the existence of God is unknowable] to hunt for her.

Darrow asked Bryan how old the earth was. Bryan replied that according to the Bible it was 5,929 years old. Darrow then confronted him with scientific and historical evidence of civilizations much older than that.

Bryan had no answer and began to get angry. "He is trying to cast ridicule on everybody who believes in the Bible," he roared.

"We have the purpose of preventing bigots and ignoramuses from controlling the education of the United States!" Darrow snapped back.

The crowd began to grow silent as Darrow continued to pick apart the strict interpretation of the Bible, in the process getting Bryan to give ridiculous answers. Darrow got Bryan to say that women's labor pains in childbirth were not biological but were instead caused by Eve's tempting of Adam with the apple in the

Substitute teacher John Scopes listens to his sentence, a $100 fine. In reality, Scopes had never actually taught evolution, the crime for which he was convicted.

Garden of Eden. The crowd grew quieter.

Darrow then got Bryan to say that the snake in the Garden of Eden had to crawl "on his belly" ever since for his role in the apple incident.

> Darrow: Do you think that is why the serpent is compelled to crawl on his belly?
> Bryan: I believe that.
> Darrow: Have you any idea how the snake went before that time?
> Bryan: No, sir.
> Darrow: Do you know whether he walked on his tail or not?
> Bryan: No, sir. I have no way to know.

At that, the crowd began to laugh loudly. Later, Bryan stammered through questions on the creation of the world and finally admitted that it probably took millions of years and not just six days, as he'd originally insisted. Darrow's daylong hammering of Bryan completely destroyed him (he died a week later) and weakened the idea nationwide of strict interpretation of the Bible. The next day, Darrow startled the country by changing Scopes's plea to guilty in order to stop Bryan from launching into what would have been a soaring speech to the jury. The jury, whose focus was narrowed by the judge to merely whether or not Scopes had taught evolution, found the high school teacher guilty. He was fined $100.

Although Scopes was technically guilty, the Fundamentalist religious movement to stop the teaching of evolution was slowed considerably. The law prohibiting the teaching of evolution itself remained on the books in Tennessee for many years but was never tested again. More than 40 states considered similar laws over the next decade, but only a handful passed them and they were never enforced. It wasn't until 1968, in *Epperson v. Arkansas*, that the United States Supreme Court ruled once and for all that no state could stop teachers from discussing evolution in schools. The courtroom battle between two famous lawyers in a small town in Tennessee during the hot summer of 1925 changed forever the roles of religion, science, and education in the United States.

The
Scottsboro Boys:
Black and
White Justice

One of the easiest ways to get from one town to another in America during the 1930s was to jump on a freight train as it rolled slowly past a junction, avoiding any railroad workers. On March 24, 1931, 12 black teenagers from Scottsboro, Alabama, did just that. But they jumped onto the wrong car of the wrong train on the wrong day. And that single train ride, which they had hoped would lead them to jobs during the leanest times of the Great Depression, led them instead into a legal and racial nightmare that ended in one of the most highly publicized series of trials in U.S. history at the height of segregation in the South.

The open-air, wooden-sided freight car the 12 youths leaped into was also occupied by Ruby Bates and Victoria Price, two young mill workers who were also prostitutes; two men traveling with them; and several other white men. The white men got into a fight with the black teenagers and were thrown off the cars, along

55

with three of the teenagers from Scottsboro, leaving just one white man, Orville Gilley, the two women, and nine of the black youths.

The men tossed from the train, some cut badly, told local police a harrowing story about being viciously assaulted by a gang of black teens. Police phoned ahead to another town on the line, where a sheriff rounded up 75 men—all white—armed them, and arrested the nine unsuspecting youths when the train stopped there.

The two women, completely dressed and showing no signs of a struggle, claimed they had been raped and were hustled off the train and taken to doctors for examination. The nine black teens were jailed on rape charges. At that time, short of murdering a white, there was no greater crime any black man could commit in the South than to rape a white woman. The alleged rapes ignited a firestorm of hatred throughout Alabama and cries that the black youths be executed.

The Scottsboro youths—Haywood Patterson, Olen Montgomery, Clarence Norris, Willie Roberson, Andy Wright, Ozie Powell, Charlie Weems, Eugene Williams, and Roy Wright—were all from low-income families and were defended by two local, court-appointed attorneys in four separate trials. The trials began less than a month after the incident took place, and the attoneys had no time to prepare a defense, as they were assigned to the youths on the first day of the trials.

At trial, the alleged victims stuck to the same story: They were held down at knifepoint and raped by all the black youths. Several white men testified that they saw the defendants holding the girls down as the train passed by. Doctors who examined the women just after they got off the train testified that the women had had sex recently. Little was made of the doctors' other testimony—that there were no obvious signs of rape.

Defense attorneys were not allowed to tell the jury that the two women slept with their traveling compan-

Alleged rape victim Victoria Price testifies at the retrial of Haywood Patterson, April 4, 1933. Ruby Bates, the other alleged victim, had already admitted that no rapes ever occurred, but Price stuck to her original story, and Patterson was again convicted.

ions the night before, either. The defendants denied everything. The judge, Alf Hawkins, moved the trials along quickly; they were over in three days. Each of the Scottsboro teens was found guilty by an all-white jury and all but the youngest were sentenced to die in the electric chair. As each verdict was announced, the all-white crowd gathered outside the courthouse on a sloping green lawn sang "There'll Be a Hot Time in the Old Town Tonight."

The quick trials and death sentences in a very suspicious looking case brought on a storm of publicity across the country and prompted the International Labor Defense (ILD), an arm of the Communist Party, to take over the cases of the "Scottsboro Boys," as the world press now called them. The ILD staged massive public rallies all over the world to protest the verdict. The ILD also sent the mothers of the boys on speaking tours throughout the United States, which drew large crowds and more press attention. Tens of thousands of Americans, including some of the most prominent people in the country, signed petitions to free the Scottsboro Boys. An ILD plea to the Alabama Supreme Court was fruitless, but the U.S. Supreme Court did order new trials, presided over by a new judge, James Horton, Jr.

The case took a bizarre turn when Ruby Bates wrote a letter to a boyfriend in which she admitted that all of her testimony was false and that she was never raped. The boys and their new attorney, New Yorker Sam Leibowitz, were convinced they could win the second trials, which started in late March 1933 with the trial of Haywood Patterson. They were able to question the two men who slept with the women the night before the alleged gang rape and got them to admit that they had sex with the women. Then Ruby Bates, who had changed her entire story, took the stand, and the courtroom grew silent.

> Leibowitz: You testified at each of the trials at Scottsboro, didn't you?
>
> Bates: Yes.
>
> Leibowitz: You said you saw six Negroes rape Victoria Price and six raped you, didn't you?
>
> Bates: Yes, but I was excited when I told it.
>
> Leibowitz: You told at Scottsboro that one held a knife at your throat, and what happened to you was just the same that happened to Victoria Price. Did someone tell you to say that?
>
> Bates: Victoria Price told me to say that.

Protestors demanding the release of the Scottsboro Boys take their case to the gates of the White House, May 8, 1933. Haywood Patterson's mother, Janine, is in the center of the photo, next to the child. Her son would remain in prison for another 15 years.

Leibowitz: Did she say what would happen if you didn't do as you were told?

Bates: Yes, she said we might have to lay out a sentence in jail.

Price, however, refused to change her story and insisted that both she and Bates were raped.

The jurors needed 22 hours to come to a verdict this time, but it was exactly the same: guilty. The second verdict angered millions across the country and turned the case into a cauldron of racism, Communist-bashing, and anti-Semitism. Leibowitz, returning to New York, called the jurors "bigots whose mouths are slits in their faces, whose eyes popped out at you like frogs, whose chins dripped with tobacco juice, bewhiskered and filthy. . . ." The prosecutor said all Leibowitz wanted was "Jew justice." Thousands in the South screamed that the Communists, who defended the boys, were trying to take over America.

The ILD once again staged a series of rallies and parades, this time led by none other than Ruby Bates. She even led a march of tens of thousands of people through the streets of Washington, D.C., and, with the boys' mothers, tried unsuccessfully to see President Roosevelt. Public opinion in the North was, once again, on the side of the boys, but it had shifted significantly in the South. By 1933 most of the editors of the South's major newspapers had changed their minds about the case and insisted that the boys should be freed. The *Richmond News Leader* even wrote in an editorial: "The men are being sentenced to death primarily because they are black. . . ."

Southerners who found that hard to accept were jolted two months later when Judge Horton, unable to keep still any longer, announced that he was throwing out the guilty verdict because it was clear to him that Price was lying and that no rapes took place. It did little good. Haywood Patterson was convicted again at a third trial, at the end of 1933, and the other boys were also convicted—all by white juries.

The Supreme Court again stepped in to the case in April 1935, throwing out all the verdicts and ordering new trials, this time because blacks were barred from grand juries in the counties where the trials were held. It didn't matter. Patterson, Norris, Weems, and the others were convicted again by yet another all-white jury. The sentences were lighter this time. Norris was again sentenced to death, but Patterson was given 75 years; Andy Wright, 99 years; Weems, 75 years; and Powell, 20 years.

The Scottsboro injustice had run its course by then, however, and it seemed clear to everyone—black and white—that the boys were innocent. The prosecutor decided to drop all charges against the four youngest defendants in 1936; they were pardoned in 1937. Alabama's governor, Bibb Graves, agreed to free the five remaining boys at the end of 1937 but changed his mind, and the last of them, Haywood Patterson, remained in prison until his escape in 1948.

Ironically, the long effort of public officials, prosecutors, and white juries to execute the Scottsboro Boys, and thereby keep the South's blacks "in their place," backfired. The enormous worldwide outcry over the trials was an important factor in the later integration of the South.

The Lindbergh Kidnapping Trial: Who Killed the Little Boy?

Aviator Charles Lindbergh and his wife, poet Anne Morrow Lindbergh, pose in front of their plane during an airline-inspection tour. Lindbergh's 1927 solo transatlantic flight, the first ever, made him a national hero. He used his celebrity to influence the investigation into his son's kidnapping and death—at the expense, many believe, of uncovering what really happened.

During the early evening of March 1, 1932, someone climbed a ladder to a second-story window of the New Jersey mansion of aviator Charles Lindbergh, the first man to fly solo across the Atlantic Ocean. The person entered the nursery and kidnapped Lindbergh's two-year-old son, Charlie Jr. Within hours of the discovery, dozens of reporters were wedged into the living room of the house, police in three states had set up roadblocks, and hundreds of curiosity seekers began to arrive, tramping through the lawns and forests around the estate. By morning, the kidnapping had become a front-page story across the world. The investigation and trial were the most highly publicized in history up to that time.

The kidnapping of the Lindbergh baby shocked the country. Rumors flew, and the biggest was that an organized-crime family had taken the child. For years, many would insist that the man convicted of the crime was not the kidnapper but that one of Lindbergh's trusted

Investigators demonstrate how the kidnapper gained entry to the second-floor nursery of the Lindbergh mansion. After the crime, the ladder was found in nearby woods.

servants was, or that the man convicted had accomplices. People also said that in his efforts to head up the investigation—something he could do only because of his fame—Lindbergh ruined whatever chances the police had to get to the bottom of the case.

Police investigators, led by New Jersey State Police superintendent H. Norman Schwarzkopf (the father of General Norman Schwarzkopf, who led American forces in the Gulf War in 1991), at first had few clues. They found a man's muddy footprints in the ground beneath the baby's window, located a homemade ladder in the woods nearby, had a badly written ransom note requesting $50,000 for the return of the child, discovered the tire tracks of two cars on a road near the mansion, and had reports from several neighbors that either one or two large cars had been seen driving in the area at the time of the kidnapping.

The crowd of neighbors and curiosity seekers who trudged all over the grounds of the estate wiped out any chance for the police to do a complete job of checking the area for evidence and footprints. They were unable to arrest the kidnapper, as they had hoped, through a man called "Graveyard John," who collected the ransom money, and Lindbergh himself refused to help them at times. The police were under intense pressure from the press and public during the two-year investigation, especially after the baby's body was found on May 12, 1932.

The police had told Lindbergh to pay the ransom in gold certificates. A few months later, the U.S. government called in gold certificates, making them rare. The police then tracked gold certificates passed in the New York area, hoping they would turn up some whose serial numbers matched those of certificates paid as ransom, and that this might lead them to the kidnapper. They finally got lucky when a man paid for gas with a gold certificate and the gas station attendant, who was concerned that banks might no longer be accepting gold certificates, took down the license number of the man's car. Police suspected that this man was the kidnapper and killer. They tracked the car to a German immigrant with a police record for robbery named Bruno Richard Hauptmann. He was arrested on September 15, 1934, despite pleas from his wife, Anna, that he was innocent.

Over 200 reporters and 100 photographers converged on the tiny town of Flemington, New Jersey, for the trial. They couldn't believe what they saw. On the very first day, more than 100,000 people jammed the narrow main street of the town, somehow hoping to get into the small courtroom. Hundreds of police had to be hired to hold them back. Traffic was tied up for miles. Getting into the spirit of the spectacle, Flemington restaurants featured dishes commemorating the case's principals. One hotel offered a "Lindbergh Sundae";

another, a "Hauptmann Pudding."

The courtroom itself was like a circus. Reporters jammed the balcony and benches to take notes, and photographers were allowed to snap pictures during the trial. (This proved so disruptive that afterward cameras were banned in all U.S. courts and didn't return for 60 years.) The crowd in the courtroom cheered whenever Lindbergh arrived or left, and autograph seekers chased him through the halls. Police advised him to wear a gun under his coat in case someone tried to kill him. Spectators brought sandwiches and bottles of soda, and some even spread blankets and tablecloths on benches and had picnics during testimony. The rich and famous who attended each day included movie and radio stars, such as Jack Benny.

In a practice that later became common, Anna Hauptmann sold her story to the *New York American* newspaper for $25,000 so she could hire an attorney for her husband. Several reporters immediately wrote books about the case, and the affair also launched political careers for some involved.

The prosecutor, David Wilentz, argued that Hauptmann, acting alone, kidnapped the baby and that the baby died accidentally when dropped from the ladder. Hauptmann then fled with the body, which he dumped off a highway near Mount Rose, New Jersey. Despite his knowledge that the baby was dead, Hauptmann asked for and received the ransom.

The case against Hauptmann appeared strong. Police claimed that the homemade ladder found near the Lindbergh estate (which contained a section of wood previously used for indoor construction) was identical to a sketch of a ladder discovered in Hauptmann's notebook, that tool marks on the ladder matched Hauptmann's tools, and that the section of indoor wood matched a sawed-off section of planking in Hauptmann's attic. Hauptmann's handwriting, experts testified, was identical to the handwriting on the ran-

TAKEN GOOD CARE OF

LOOK FOR. INSTRUCTIONS SATURDAY. IF POLICE GET TO CLOSE LOOK OUT

POST CARD

ADDRESS

CHAS. LINBERG HOPEWELL N. J RUSH

This poorly written communication, postmarked two days after the kidnapping, was said to be in the hand of Bruno Richard Hauptmann.

som notes. The man who gave the mysterious "Graveyard John" the ransom money at a New York cemetery testified that "John" was Hauptmann, and Lindbergh himself, who was in hiding within earshot when the ransom was paid, said "John's" voice was that of Hauptmann. In addition, several eyewitnesses identified him as the man passing the gold certificates, and police found almost $15,000 in certificates in his garage.

Hauptmann offered an explanation for why he had the gold certificates. He said that a friend and business partner named Isidor Fisch had asked him to keep a shoe box and that when Fisch died while on a trip to Europe, he had opened the box, which contained the certificates. Because Fisch had owed him money, Hauptmann claimed, he began passing the certificates. Hauptmann's lawyers also pointed to weaknesses in the prosecution's case. For example, the section of wood in the ladder that was said to have come from Hauptmann's attic was about six and a half feet long.

Charles Lindbergh on the witness stand at the trial of Bruno Richard Hauptmann. Lindbergh testified that he recognized Hauptmann's voice as that of "Graveyard John," the man who collected the ransom money.

Yet the missing section from the attic was eight feet long. Would Hauptmann, a professional carpenter, have mismeasured by such a large amount? And why would he have needed to cut wood from his attic in the first place?

Nevertheless, it didn't take the jury long to return a guilty verdict. Hauptmann was sentenced to death.

As soon as the trial ended, however, many people began to wonder whether Hauptmann might be innocent or, if not, whether he had really acted alone. Kidnappers seldom worked alone (one guarded the victim while the other collected the money). How could a kidnapper know so much about the Lindbergh house, and the comings and goings of the family, unless he worked

Bruno Hauptmann (right) confers with his lead attorney, Edward J. Reilly, during his trial for the kidnapping and killing of the Lindbergh baby. Prosecutors maintained that Hauptmann, acting alone, committed the crime, but doubts persist.

with someone on the inside? How could Hauptmann have acted alone if there were tire marks from two cars on the Lindbergh estate that night? Several eyewitnesses saw two cars racing down local streets that night as well. Why was one of the Lindberghs' chauffeurs spending a lot of money right after the ransom was paid? Why did two potential witnesses commit suicide? Why did another flee the country and disappear? And where was the nearly $30,000 in ransom money that was unaccounted for?

If there was more than one kidnapper, Lindbergh was largely responsible for preventing his or her capture. He insisted right from the start that one man kidnapped and murdered his son, and rejected all talk about a conspiracy. He refused to let police interview servants at his home or at his mother-in-law's, refused to permit a polygraph (lie detector) test for servants, and would not listen to police theories about multiple kidnappers.

After several unsuccessful appeals and a 30-day reprieve, Hauptmann was executed on April 3, 1936. But doubts about the case have lingered. Several law school classes that studied the case agreed that more than one kidnapper was involved. An investigative reporter concluded that Hauptmann was totally innocent and had been framed by police. In 1983 Michael Baden, a renowned New York City medical examiner, studied the baby's autopsy report and concluded that the child did not die accidentally but was probably shot. Until she died, Anna Hauptmann swore that her husband was innocent and that he was arrested because of the general anti-German feeling in the 1930s tied to the rise of Adolf Hitler and the Nazis.

Was Bruno Hauptmann an innocent man framed for the crime by others? Did Hauptmann commit the kidnapping by himself? Did he have accomplices? Only Hauptmann could tell the entire story, and he's dead.

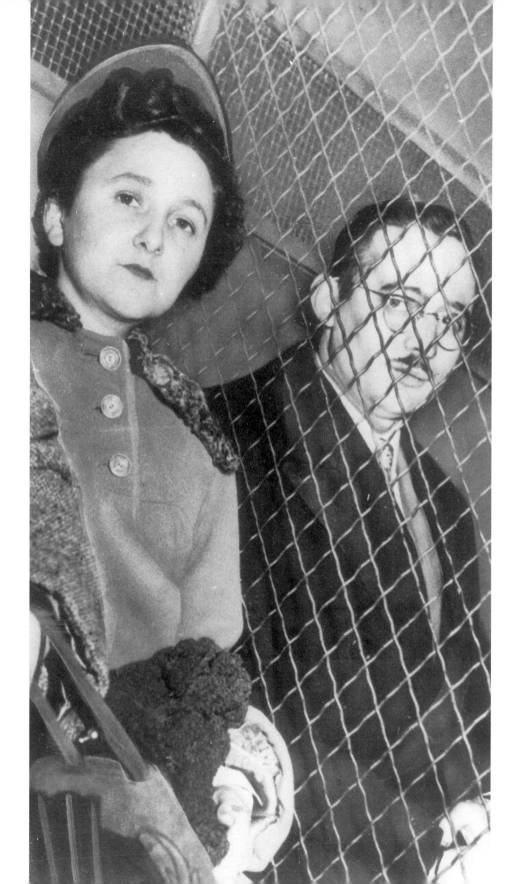

THE ROSENBERGS, THE RUSSIANS, AND THE ATOMIC BOMB

orld War II came to an end after the United States dropped two atomic bombs on the Japanese cities of Hiroshima and Nagasaki in August 1945. The powerful new weapons gave America military superiority over every other nation.

Then, in 1949, Americans were stunned when they learned that the Soviet Union, a wartime ally that was emerging as a bitter enemy, had tested its own atomic bomb. The United States no longer had a monopoly on atomic weapons.

American scientists and military leaders couldn't understand how the Soviet Union had managed to produce a bomb years before intelligence sources had predicted. The decoding of secret Soviet cables put investigators on a trail that led to the explanation: espionage. The Soviets had managed to recruit spies and infiltrate various industrial and research centers in England, Canada, and the United States, including the

73

Los Alamos, New Mexico, complex where America's atom bomb was designed and developed.

The most prominent atomic spy was Klaus Fuchs, a German-born physicist who worked with the British delegation to Los Alamos and had access to a great deal of key information. Piecing together clues from various sources, agents from the Federal Bureau of Investigation identified Fuchs as a prime suspect in September 1949 and alerted British authorities (Fuchs had since returned to England). In January 1950 he confessed, and in March he was convicted of espionage and sentenced to 14 years in prison by a British court.

Soon, dozens of other people were implicated in Canada, England, and the United States. Among them were two New Yorkers: an electrical engineer named Julius Rosenberg, arrested on July 17, and his wife, Ethel, arrested on August 11. The Rosenbergs were accused of being atomic-espionage ringleaders. Their trial, and what happened to them afterward, attracted worldwide attention and severely tested the fairness of the American court system.

Julius Rosenberg had gotten a job as a civilian engineer for the U.S. Army Signal Corps in 1940, and by 1942 he may have been providing information to the Soviet Union and recruiting spies. But the Rosenbergs weren't involved in atomic espionage until 1944—if they were involved at all. In August of that year, Ethel Rosenberg's younger brother, David Greenglass, an army machinist, was assigned to Los Alamos. When Greenglass's wife, Ruth, traveled to New Mexico in late 1944 to visit her husband, she allegedly carried a request from Julius Rosenberg: He wanted the young machinist to provide him with information on America's atomic-bomb program. After thinking about it, Greenglass, who had been unaware of the full scope of Los Alamos's mission, agreed.

During a January 1945 furlough, Greenglass claimed, he supplied his brother-in-law with informa-

Emblem of angst: The mushroom cloud from an atomic explosion rises above the desert in Yucca Flat, Nevada, while GIs participating in military exercises look on. Following the Soviet Union's successful test of an atom bomb in August 1949, American military planners and civilians had to contemplate the unthinkable: nuclear war. Were the Rosenbergs scapegoats of the troubled times? Many observers said yes.

tion about his work, including sketches of explosive molds, which were critical to the success of the plutonium bomb (the type dropped on Nagasaki). Rosenberg then instructed him to gather more information and told him that someone would travel to New Mexico later to pick that information up. Cutting a Jello box top in half, he gave one piece to Greenglass and said that the person assigned to pick up the information would present the other piece as a recognition signal.

In June 1945, two months before the atomic bombings of Hiroshima and Nagasaki, an American chemist named Harry Gold showed up at the Albuquerque, New Mexico, apartment of David and Ruth Greenglass. For several years Gold had been an espionage courier, meeting Klaus Fuchs and taking documents back to his Russian control (the agent who supervised his activities). On this occasion Gold told Greenglass, "Julius sent me," and when Greenglass produced half a Jello box top, he took out the matching piece. Greenglass then turned over an envelope full of atomic-bomb secrets and told Gold he could contact him in New York through his brother-in-law Julius.

In 1950, when the spy scandal was made public, Julius and Ethel Rosenberg, Harry Gold, David Greenglass, and a number of others were arrested for espionage. Gold and Greenglass pleaded guilty and were given prison sentences. The Rosenbergs insisted they were innocent and went to trial.

The Rosenbergs, who had two small children, seemed unlikely international spies. Ethel was a short, slight woman, just five feet tall and weighing less than 100 pounds, with a round, attractive face. Julius was a tall, thin man with jet black hair and a pencil-thin mustache who wore wire-frame glasses. Although the government charged that they were paid money by the Russians for the atomic bomb's secrets, they had lived modestly in a tiny New York apartment for years. The couple, married 11 years, held hands throughout much of the trial, which began in March 1951 in New York.

The Rosenbergs' trial took place against a backdrop of intense fear and hatred of Communism. In 1950 North Korea, backed by the Soviet Union and China, had invaded South Korea, and now war raged between the Communist forces and a U.S.-led United Nations coalition determined to repel them. In Europe a tense standoff existed between the Soviet Union and the United States and its allies; many Americans were convinced that the Russians wanted to bring all of Western Europe under their influence. On the home front, Senator Joseph McCarthy was conducting hearings to ferret out the supposed Communists and Communist sympathizers in the State Department, and a congressional committee was formed to root out Communists in the film industry. Most troubling of all, however, was the thought that America's enemy could now unleash the power of the atom and destroy entire cities.

This anti-Communist climate colored the case against the Rosenbergs. Both were longtime members of the American Communist Party and both had demonstrated publicly for Communist issues. To many people, including some newspaper columnists, this made them evil, and the Rosenbergs became symbols of the worldwide Communist threat.

Irving Saypol, the lead prosecutor in the case, reinforced this climate with out-of-court comments—made during the trial—about the damage the Rosenbergs had done. Judge Irving Kaufman, who clearly favored the prosecution and may have been angling for a nomination to the Supreme Court, even communicated with the FBI and the Justice Department during the trial, a gross ethical lapse.

The government produced a parade of witnesses who charged that the Rosenbergs asked them to turn over atomic secrets, which they would then transmit to the Russians. Max Elitcher, a college friend of Julius Rosenberg's who worked for the navy, testified that Julius and another man, Morton Sobell, who was on trial with the Rosenbergs, attempted to get him to sell secrets to the Russians. Later, he said, Sobell asked him to recruit college students as Soviet spies, and he accompanied Sobell when Sobell gave a secret film of some kind to Julius Rosenberg.

The testimony of David Greenglass was the most damaging. Greenglass claimed that the Rosenbergs told his wife they were Soviet spies and wanted Greenglass to turn over bomb secrets to them for the Russians. He was paid several thousand dollars for the information he provided. Greenglass told the court that he had given Harry Gold—who he said worked for his brother-in-law—secrets, including actual sketches for the bomb, which later wound up in Russian hands.

Harry Gold testified that he had met with the noto-

He provided the Soviets with crucial technical information about America's nuclear program, but physicist Klaus Fuchs (pictured here) received only a 14-year prison term. Of all those convicted in the atomic-espionage case, only the Rosenbergs were sentenced to death.

Admitted spies Harry Gold (left) and David Greenglass. The Rosenbergs' defense attorneys claimed that the testimony of these two men, the prosecution's star witnesses, was motivated by the promise of reduced sentences.

rious convicted spy Klaus Fuchs, giving substantial weight to his testimony. He added that when he met with the Greenglasses in Albuquerque he was told to say he "was from Julius."

Elizabeth Bentley, a Communist Party member and admitted espionage courier, testified that while she waited in a car, her Russian control visited the apartment of an engineer in the same neighborhood where the Rosenbergs lived. In addition, she received several phone calls from a man named "Julius" who said that he wanted to see her control and asked that she relay the message.

The Rosenbergs were defended by the father-and-son team of Alex and Emanuel H. Bloch. E. H. Bloch presented a careful defense that attempted to show the jury that all of the evidence against his clients was circumstantial. (Circumstantial evidence is evidence that does not prove the fact in contention but merely provides a reasonable basis for believing it to be true.)

Gold, as an example, never met Julius Rosenberg. Bentley never knew that the "Julius" she spoke with by telephone was Julius Rosenberg.

Bloch saved his most scathing attack for Greenglass. He said that any man who would testify against his own sister and brother-in-law had to have a secret reason. He then showed that Greenglass had become a business partner of Julius Rosenberg after the war and, in a deal involving their company's stock, felt he had been cheated. Greenglass then tried to borrow several thousand dollars from Julius and was turned down. He admitted that one night he screamed at Julius, ". . . if you don't get me that money you are going to be sorry!" The lawyer also argued, again and again, that Greenglass was making up a story about Rosenberg in order to get himself a lighter sentence and that he was the true traitor to the United States.

The Rosenbergs took the stand and denied that they were involved in spying, but they didn't deny that they were longtime members of the Communist Party. They were branded Communists in the news media every day, and soon the connections between the Communists, the Soviets, and the Rosenbergs became a blur.

Defense lawyer E. H. Bloch delivered a powerful summation to the jury in which he tore apart the evidence against the Rosenbergs and asked the jury how two meek-looking people living in a tiny apartment without any money could be the masterminds of an international spy ring. Then he got to the heart of the matter—that the case was not about spying, but about politics:

> Please don't decide this case because you may have some bias or some prejudice against some political philosophy. . . . If you want to convict these defendants because you think they are Communists and you don't like any member of the Communist party, then, ladies and gentlemen, I can sit down now and there is absolutely no use in my talking. . . . That is not the crime.

His argument did little good. The jury found the Rosenbergs guilty. But that was not the most surprising development. The real surprise came when Judge Kaufman sentenced them to be executed, even though everyone else charged with the same crimes received prison terms and even though no American court had ever sentenced a civilian to die for spying (no court has since). "I consider your crime worse than murder," said the judge.

> I believe your conduct in putting into the hands of the Russians the A-bomb, years before our best scientists predicted Russia would perfect the bomb, has already caused . . . Communist aggression in Korea, with the resultant casualties exceeding fifty thousand and who knows but what that millions more innocent people may pay the price of your treason.

Judge Kaufman's use of the word *treason* was inflammatory and, legally speaking, inaccurate. The Rosenbergs had been convicted of espionage. When their alleged crimes took place, the United States and the Soviet Union were allies in the war against Nazi Germany. Therefore, it couldn't be said that they were attempting to overthrow the U.S. government.

Nevertheless, the sentence stood. What followed was a three-year-long drama as E. H. Bloch, who brought the Rosenbergs' two children to death row to visit them regularly, filed 19 different appeals to get them a new trial or a reduced sentence.

There was public drama too, as millions of people around the world, outraged at the verdict and sentence, demonstrated to free the Rosenbergs or keep them from the electric chair. Many felt that the anti-Communist hysteria in the United States was responsible for the verdicts and harsh sentencing and that in another era the Rosenbergs would have gone free or received jail terms. Many others argued that the fact that the Rosenbergs were Jewish played a role. Thousands of petitions were sent to Presidents Harry S. Truman

and Dwight D. Eisenhower and to other government officials. Marches were held and over $1 million was collected for a legal fund.

Their lawyers managed to win several stays of execution for the couple, keeping them alive for three years. But finally, just days before they were scheduled to die, the U.S. Supreme Court, by a 5-4 vote, upheld their conviction and execution. They were electrocuted on June 19, 1953, to the end maintaining their innocence.

The death chamber at Sing Sing, where Julius and Ethel Rosenberg were electrocuted on June 19, 1953. No American civilians had ever been executed for espionage, and none have been since.

THE VIETNAM
WAR AND THE
CHICAGO SEVEN

The 1960s was a troubled decade for America. The United States and the Soviet Union almost went to war over Berlin and then Cuba. Poverty reached new levels. The civil rights movement evoked heated passions and often sparked violence, and race riots devastated the Watts section of Los Angeles, Detroit, and Newark, New Jersey. Assassins cut down President John F. Kennedy, civil rights leader Martin Luther King, Jr., and Senator Robert Kennedy, who was running for president. And in the jungles and rice paddies of Vietnam, American soldiers were dying in a war that was becoming increasingly unpopular on the home front.

The 1960s was also the decade in which American youth, particularly college students, became a powerful

Police battle antiwar demonstrators in the streets of Chicago. A few blocks from the melee, the Democratic National Convention was in the process of selecting the party's 1968 presidential nominee.

force in politics, staging protest marches and demonstrations in support of civil rights and against the Vietnam War. College students from coast to coast marched through city streets, seized college administration buildings, campaigned for antiwar political candidates, and held large public rallies. These protests were effective. In 1965 Congress passed sweeping new legislation to guarantee the rights of black Americans and began a war on poverty. And antiwar protests contributed to President Lyndon Johnson's decision not to seek reelection in 1968.

The war in Vietnam continued, however. Opponents of the war decided that the most public way to protest was to hold huge demonstrations during the 1968 Democratic National Convention in Chicago.

Trouble seemed guaranteed when the city of Chicago, hit with race riots in 1966 and in the spring of 1968, refused to give the protestors permits to gather in city parks or to hold marches. City officials announced that protestors would be surrounded by police with special riot gear—as if to dare antiwar protestors to do something.

The inevitable clash came on Sunday night, August 25, when a small army of helmeted police moved through Lincoln Park, pushing and shoving protestors into the streets, clubbing and punching many, even hitting young women on the ground. Many students began cursing at the police, which provoked even more beatings. The park sweeps occurred again on Monday, Tuesday, and Wednesday. Hundreds of protestors were injured by the police, who again used clubs on the students. At one point police pushed a group of students backward, causing many to fall through plate glass windows in a downtown department store.

The protests and beatings were seen on national television, and leading politicians from the Democratic Party in the convention hall denounced the police's tactics, but city police continued to halt demonstra-

tions with force for the next several days.

Later, the Walker Commission, a national group that investigated the Chicago demonstrations, concluded that the police, not the protestors, were at fault and called the situation "a police riot." Chicago officials, angered by the report, struck back and presented the protest case to a grand jury, which indicted most of the leaders of the marches for inciting a riot. They were all well-known anti–Vietnam War protestors: David Dellinger, Rennie Davis, Tom Hayden, Abbie Hoffman, Jerry Rubin, Lee Weiner, John Froines, and Bobby Seale (a leader of the Black Panthers, a militant black political organization). And they saw their trials as an opportunity to publicize their views.

The group, dubbed the "Chicago Eight" by the press, arrived in court in July 1969 for what turned into one of the most bizarre trials in American history, a trial in which freedom of speech and protest was pitted against public safety. The confrontations that came

American soldiers ford a river near Da Nang, South Vietnam. Opposition to U.S. involvement in the Vietnam War polarized the nation and became a source of increasing government concern. The Chicago Seven saw their trial as a political vendetta and an attempt by the government to silence their antiwar message.

later were set up quickly when the judge, 73-year-old Julius Hoffman—who was known for progovernment rulings—promptly refused all of the defendants' pretrial motions, including a plea to make public the government's wiretaps of their phone calls, and ordered four of the defense lawyers not in court on the first day jailed if they didn't show up the following morning. Then one of the jurors was excused after she received a death threat signed by the Black Panther Party (the defense claimed that the threat was a fake).

The actual trial began after that wobbly start. The government's case was based on the testimony of several undercover police officers and a journalism student who testified that the defendants urged demonstrators to riot—and that was what triggered the protests police had to put down. A tape was played on which Seale was heard to say: "If the police get in the way of our march . . . kill them and send them to the morgue slab."

The defense countered that the witnesses were lying and that, regardless, freedom of speech permitted the defendants to say what they wanted, although they had never urged followers to riot. Representing the defendants was a team of lawyers led by William Kunstler, who frequently defended men and women in political trials.

The trial quickly heated up when Bobby Seale repeatedly claimed that none of the lawyers represented him and insisted that he be allowed to represent himself. An angry Judge Hoffman kept denying his motion, and Seale began calling the judge a "racist," a "pig," and a "fascist." The judge ordered that Seale be gagged and tied to his chair. The trial continued, with Seale bound and gagged, but was continually stopped because through the gag Seale kept oinking. Seale was finally sent back to his jail cell to be tried separately, but not before Judge Hoffman found him guilty of contempt and sentenced him to four years in prison (a harsh sentence).

Seale's sentence triggered chaos in the court. The other defendants started to shout and yell in the courtroom, often laughing whenever the judge made a ruling. They refused to rise when the judge entered. They brought Viet Cong flags to court and one day even dressed up in black judges' robes. Unruly spectators who cheered whenever the defendants entered were routinely removed. Hoffman eventually charged the remaining seven defendants, now the Chicago Seven, with a record 159 counts of contempt.

The atmosphere outside the courthouse was compared to a circus. Six of the defendants were free on bail and held press conferences every day at which they denounced the judge and the federal government. They flew to far-off cities on weekends to lead antiwar marches and rallies, generating enormous publicity,

Jerry Rubin (seated) holds a press conference following his release from jail, October 8, 1969. Standing behind him are his Chicago Seven codefendants. From left: Abbie Hoffman, John Froines, Lee Weiner, David Dellinger, Rennie Davis, and Tom Hayden.

On the final day of the Chicago Seven trial, renowned defense attorney William Kunstler (above) decried "a steadily increasing governmental encroachment upon [Americans'] most fundamental liberties."

much of it favorable, in an effort to show that the government was unfairly trying them in order to stop the antiwar movement.

On the final day of the trial, the defense lawyers denounced the government's attacks on the protestors' rights. Said William Kunstler:

> I can only hope that my fate does not deter other lawyers throughout the country who, in the difficult days that lie ahead, will be asked to defend clients against a steadily increasing governmental encroachment upon their most fundamental liberties. . . . I dread to contemplate the future domestic and foreign course of this country.

The jury, following the judge's direction—which the defense lawyers called biased—found the defendants guilty. Before sentencing, Hoffman asked the defendants if they had anything to say. They certainly did.

"You see us on trial in a criminal case," defendant Lee Weiner told the judge. "We see ourselves under the gun of a political trial being used as a weapon in the hands of the government in an ongoing political war against dissent and youth in this country."

Dellinger said Hoffman was "misguided and intolerant" and compared him with King George III of England at the time of the American Revolution. "You are trying to hold back the tide of history, but you will not succeed," he concluded.

Abbie Hoffman, one of the most outrageous defendants in speech and dress, laughed at the judge again and said, "Julius, you radicalized more young people than we ever could. You're the country's top Yippie!" (The Yippies—members of the Youth International Party—were a counterculture group opposed to the war.)

The judge smiled and then imposed the maximum sentence of five years in prison for each defendant, calling the men "dangerous people."

But the Chicago Seven remained free on bail, leading protest after protest, while their lawyers appealed the trial through several courts, charging that it had been a political vendetta. Finally, an appellate court threw out the verdict, saying that Judge Hoffman had frequently acted improperly, and ordered a new trial for Seale on his contempt sentence—but only if the government let him look at its wiretaps. New trials were ordered for the Chicago Seven on the contempt charges.

In the end, the government dropped all the charges against Bobby Seale, who went free. The government did bring the Chicago Seven to trial on their 159 contempt charges before Judge Edward Gignoux of Maine, but not for three more years. He found them guilty but didn't impose any sentence. None of the protestors ever went to prison.

Although the legal outcome of the trial was muddled, it received so much coverage in the press, with the judicial system and government painted as villains, that the antiwar movement became stronger because of it. Finally, in 1975, after years of public protest, the last American troops left Vietnam.

Further Reading

1. HYSTERIA: THE WITCHES OF SALEM

Conde, Maryse. *Tituba, Black Witch of Salem*. Charlottesville: University of Virginia Press, 1992.

Dickler, Gerald. *Man on Trial*. New York: Dell Publishing, 1962.

Jackson, Shirley. *The Witchcraft of Salem Village*. New York: Random House, 1956.

Petry, Ann. *Tituba of Salem Village*. New York: Crowell, 1964.

Rosenthal, Bernard. *Salem Story: Reading the Witch Trials of 1692*. Cambridge, England: Cambridge University Press, 1995.

Starkey, Marion. *The Devil in Massachusetts*. New York: Alfred A. Knopf, 1949.

2. THE COURT-MARTIAL OF BENEDICT ARNOLD

Boylan, Brian. *Benedict Arnold: The Dark Eagle*. New York: W. W. Norton Co., 1973.

Brandt, Clare. *The Man in the Mirror: A Life of Benedict Arnold*. New York: Random House, 1994.

Decker, Malcolm. *Benedict Arnold: Son of the Havens*. Tarrytown, N.Y.: William Abbott Publishers, 1932.

Donovan, Frank. *The Brave Traitor*. New York: A. S. Barnes, 1961.

Flexner, James. *The Traitor and the Spy: Benedict Arnold and John André*. New York: William Morrow & Co., 1990.

Randall, William Sterne. *Benedict Arnold: Patriot and Traitor*. New York: William Morrow & Co., 1990.

3. WHO "FIXED" THE WORLD SERIES?

Asinof, Eliot. *Eight Men Out*. New York: Henry Holt, 1987.

Frommer, Harvey. *Shoeless Joe and Ragtime Baseball*. Dallas: Taylor Publishing, 1992.

Kinsella, W. P. *Shoeless Joe*. Boston: Houghton-Mifflin, 1982.

Kavanagh, Jack. *Shoeless Joe Jackson*. New York: Chelsea House, 1995.

Luhrs, Victor. *The Great Baseball Mystery—The 1919 World Series*. New York: A. S. Barnes, 1966.

4. THE GREAT MONKEY TRIAL

Brumbaugh, Robert, ed. *Six Trials*. New York: Crowell, 1969.

Cherny, Robert. *A Righteous Cause: The Life of William Jennings Bryan*. Boston: Little, Brown & Co., 1985.

DeCamp, L. Sprague. *The Great Monkey Trial*. Garden City, N.Y.: Doubleday, 1968.

Dickler, Gerald, ed. *Man on Trial*. New York: Delta Books, 1962.

Gurko, Miriam. *Clarence Darrow*. New York: Crowell, 1965.

Hariman, Robert, ed. *Popular Trials*. Tuscaloosa: University of Alabama Press, 1990.

Levine, Lawrence. *Defender of the Faith: William Jennings Bryan—the Last Decade, 1915–1925*. New York: Oxford University Press, 1965.

Stone, Irving. *Clarence Darrow for the Defense*. New York: New American Library, 1971.

5. BLACK AND WHITE JUSTICE

Carter, Dan. *Scottsboro: A Tragedy of the American South*. Baton Rouge: Louisiana State University Press, 1969.

Hine, Darlene Clark. *The Path to Equality: From the Scottsboro Case to the Breaking of Baseball's Color Barrier, 1931–1947*. New York: Chelsea House, 1995.

Norris, Clarence. *The Last of the Scottsboro Boys*. New York: Putnam, 1979.

Patterson, Haywood, and Earl Conrad. *Scottsboro Boy*. Garden City, N.Y.: Doubleday, 1950.

6. THE LINDBERGH KIDNAPPING TRIAL

Behn, Noel. *Lindbergh: The Crime*. New York: Atlantic Monthly Press, 1994.

Dutch, Andrew. *Hysteria: Lindbergh Kidnap Case*. Philadelphia: Dorrance Publishing, 1975.

Fisher, James. *The Lindbergh Case*. New Brunswick, N.J.: Rutgers University Press, 1987.

Gill, Brendan. *Lindbergh Alone*. New York: Harcourt Brace Jovanovich, 1977.

Milton, Joyce. *Loss of Eden*. New York: HarperCollins, 1993.

Scaduto, Anthony. *Scapegoat: The Lonesome Death of Bruno Richard Hauptmann*. New York: G. P. Putnam's Sons, 1976.

7. THE ROSENBERGS

Carmichael, Virginia. *Framing History: The Rosenberg Story and the Cold War*. Minneapolis: University of Minnesota Press, 1993.

Neville, John. *The Press, the Rosenbergs and the Cold War*. Westport, Conn.: Praeger Books, 1995.

Nizer, Louis. *The Implosion Conspiracy*. Garden City, N.Y.: Doubleday, 1973.

Randolph, Ronald. *The Rosenberg File: A Search for the Truth*. New York: Holt, Rinehart & Winston, 1983.

Yalkowsky, Stan. *The Murder of the Rosenbergs*. New York: Privately Published, 1990.

8. THE CHICAGO SEVEN

Belknap, Michal, ed. *American Political Trials*. Westport, Conn.: Greenwood Press, 1994.

Hariman, Robert, ed. *Popular Trials: Rhetoric, Mass Media, and the Law*. Tuscaloosa: University of Alabama Press, 1990.

Index

BRUCE CHADWICK was a longtime reporter for the *New York Daily News* and covered many trials for that newspaper. Chadwick has written a number of books on baseball for Abbeville Press and other publishers, and his book on the rivalry of brothers during the Civil War, *Brother Against Brother*, will be published by Birch Lane this year. He is also the author of biographies of football stars Joe Namath and Deion Sanders and sports broadcaster John Madden for Chelsea House. Chadwick, an assistant professor at Jersey City State College, is completing a Ph.D. in American History at Rutgers University.

AUSTIN SARAT is William Nelson Cromwell Professor of Jurisprudence & Political Science at Amherst College, where he also chairs the Department of Law, Jurisprudence and Social Thought. Professor Sarat is the author or editor of 22 books and numerous scholarly articles. Among his books are *Law's Violence, Sitting in Judgment: Sentencing the White Collar Criminal*, and *Justice and Injustice in Law and Legal Theory*. He has received many academic awards and held several prestigious fellowships. In addition, he is a nationally recognized teacher and educator whose teaching has been featured in the *New York Times*, on the *Today* show, and on National Public Radio's *Fresh Air*.

Picture Credits

page

2:	UPI/Corbis-Bettmann	44:	UPI/Corbis-Bettmann	78:	Corbis-Bettmann
12:	AP/Wide World Photos	47:	Corbis-Bettmann	81:	AP/Wide World Photos
18-19:	Corbis-Bettmann	49:	Corbis-Bettmann	82-83:	UPI/Bettmann Newsphotos
20:	Library of Congress, #62-22032	51:	UPI/Corbis-Bettmann	85:	UPI/Corbis-Bettmann
		54:	UPI/Corbis-Bettmann	87:	UPI/Corbis-Bettmann
21:	Corbis-Bettmann	57:	UPI/Corbis-Bettmann	88:	UPI/Corbis-Bettmann
23:	Corbis-Bettmann	59:	UPI/Corbis-Bettmann		
26-27:	Corbis-Bettmann	62:	AP/Wide World Photos	Cover Photos (clockwise from bottom left): UPI/Corbis-Bettmann, AP/Wide World Photos, Corbis-Bettmann, AP/Wide Word Photos, National Baseball Library, Cooperstown, NY
28:	NYPL Picture Collection	64:	AP/Wide World Photos		
31:	Corbis-Bettmann	67:	AP/Wide World Photos		
34:	Courtesy George Brace	68-69:	AP/Wide World Photos		
37:	Chicago Historical Society	70:	AP/Wide World Photos		
39:	UPI/Corbis-Bettmann	72:	AP/Wide World Photos		
41:	National Baseball Library	75:	Corbis-Bettmann		
42:	Chicago Historical Society	77:	Corbis-Bettmann		